"Noel Sloboda's *Our Rarer Monsters* is a menagerie of myth and fairy tale and poem, but unlike the medieval bestiaries its wide-ranging offerings sometimes bring to mind, it is also grounded in the here and now, in the world we know, a place brought to new life by these smart and witty poems."

—Matt Bell,
author of *In the House upon the Dirt
between the Lake and the Woods*

"This is a world of delicious intertextualities, bold imaginings, and subtle music."

—Mihaela Moscaliuc,
author of *Father Dirt*

"People = strange monsters, and this Bates Motel–like trap of a book is where they go to die. Marc Snyder's visionary art lends more sizzle to the slippery eels of Sloboda's impressive word circus."

—Richard Peabody,
editor of *Gargoyle Magazine*

Our Rarer Monsters

Noel Sloboda

SUNNYOUTSIDE
Buffalo

Acknowledgments

Poems in this volume appeared (often in different forms) in the following periodicals: *491 Magazine, A cappella Zoo, Apt, Avocet, Centrifugal Eye, Chaffin, Commonline, Crate, Denver Syntax, Durable Goods, Euphony, Feathertale Review, Grasslimb, Haggard and Halloo, Houston Literary Review, Kansas English, Keyhole Magazine, Kill Author, Little Patuxent Review, Mad Shakespeare, Matter, Mayo Review, Modern Language Studies, Mythic Delirium, Neon, Other Poetry, Paper Crow, Petrichor Machine, Phantom Drift, Philadelphia Stories, Ping Pong, Pisgah Review, Plenum, RE:AL, Redivider, Riddle Fence, Right Hand Pointing, Roanoke Review, Rougarou, San Pedro River Review, Sein und Werden, Shakespeare Newsletter, Snail Mail Review, Sow's Ear Poetry Review, SPECS, Spillway, Superplus, Tipton Poetry Journal, U.S.1 Worksheets, Verse Wisconsin, Weave,* and *Wicked Alice.* Several of these works appeared in the chapbook *So Below.* The poem "Instructions for My Stunt Double" was included in *Feathertale's Big Book of Exquisitely Egregious Poetry and Diverse Versification and So Forth and Such.*

ISBN: 978-1-934513-39-2

Library of Congress Control Number: 2013937708

sunnyoutside
PO Box 911
Buffalo, NY 14207
USA

www.sunnyoutside.com

DANIEL, LUCA,
MAGGIE, AND
WILBUR

"MEN HEAP TOGETHER THE MISTAKES OF THEIR LIVES,
AND CREATE A MONSTER THEY CALL DESTINY."
—John Oliver Hobbes

"THE ONLY TEST, BAKER, IS HOW NOT TO ERASE
OURSELVES FROM THE MAP. OUR HISTORY IS THAT
THINGS DON'T LAST. EVERY GENERATION CREATES
THE RIGHT MONSTERS TO DESTROY ITSELF."
—Gerard Donovan,
Schopenhauer's Telescope

"NOBODY'S AFRAID OF ME ANY MORE."
—The Monster,
No Such Thing

Contents

Bequest Narrative

Every day the old man wore a different paper hat. He frequently sported some sort of bowler but sometimes donned a helmet. Every now and again, it looked as though a giant origami bird had perched atop his head. Once, we saw him in a crown with tines as long as my arm. The old man was the son of a famous librarian. This librarian had devoted his life to building a collection rumored to be the next Alexandria. He had neglected his family, focusing only on tomes and grimoires. On his deathbed, however, the collector had called his son—by then a grown man—to his bedside. The librarian had explained his choice to cherish books above all else. He insisted they had the power to make a home more durable than any physical structure: a life lived in books kept the self forever warm and dry, no matter what the season. The librarian had charged his son with caring for his library. Moments after the son had agreed, the librarian expired. The son almost immediately began to execute his duties. He established a routine: he would take one book each night, slice out the pages, then fold them into headgear for the following day. In the evening, he would burn the hat he had worn since dawn—along with the remains of yesterday's volume—working by firelight as he used a new set of pages to fashion his hat for tomorrow. By the time he wandered into our lives, the old man had burned thousands of books. While he had fuel enough to keep going through the darkest nights, he doubted he would live long enough to make it through his entire inheritance. Still, he maintained he had to try: he owed that much to his father.

Mrs. Grendel

I knew this day would come,
back when he confessed

he took his dirty laundry home
every weekend; I should have seen

he would forever be a momma's boy—
but when we first started dating

I believed I could change him.
He seemed so charming,

with that disarming smile
and throaty laugh.

So, I waxed his back, filed
his incisors, taught him a little

about vegan cooking. But none
of it mattered. An only child,

he was too used to getting
his way, always

the center of attention.
He'd go out every night,

raise hell in the mead halls,
show off for the guys.

I knew this day would come.
He'd get into fights

every other night, and I'd wake up
to find a broken sword

or a bloody head
nailed above my mantle—

him passed out on the kitchen floor.
Me? I tried to take away

his drinking money,
but his damned mother

slipped him cash on the side.
I fought to save our marriage,

signed us up for counseling;
he never showed.

I knew this day would come.
And still I say if she wasn't

in the picture, we might have
made it work. Of course

you can look—but you won't
find him here. He wouldn't

want me to see him now.
You boys will discover him

down the street, hiding out
in his mother's basement.

The Winter's Tale *Dilemma*

Nobody had warned him it would be so hard

to breathe inside the suit. As he waited
for his cue—trying to keep his paws

off himself, imagining fleas

scurrying across his hide—
he could barely

see through pinched eyes,

and the smell of his own sweat filled
his nostrils. This was not the romance

promised. Perhaps tonight,

he fantasized, he would break
from his blocking, devour

Antigonus on stage, paint the spotlights

red. But then The Mamas & the Papas started
to play; the honeyed melody

displaced the buzzing in his ears. Licking

his lips, he pirouetted onto the boards
once again: Enter bear.

Little Novelty

Baba Yaga knew she was second-string, destined for convenience stores and dollar marts. But a Pez head still meant something. The old witch felt sure she was about to arrive. When she signed the contract to license her image, Baba Yaga was full of herself. The feeling lasted for almost three months, until a package from Pez arrived. When she opened the box and spied the prototype, she was beside herself. Her limited marketability had not rated a new mold, and the company had thousands of unused candy cappers on hand from a major celebrity prematurely retired: Princess Di retained an aristocratic mien— even with her hair painted white, a great wart daubed on her nose, and two of her teeth blacked out. Baba Yaga supposed some would be flattered to have a royal likeness. Nevertheless, she cursed the Pez people, praying to long-forgotten gods that their sweet little necks would all snap.

Weasels

Coats molt and storms
follow. The landscape

flattens, as if pressed
on a great iron griddle,

making invisible the lean
gourmands only after living

meals, while everything else
rehearses slowly dying.

Advice from an Opossum

Ignore your brothers and sisters
until you secure your place
in the pouch. Then grow up quickly.

Once you step out on your own,
devour everything in your path,
from acorns to carrion. Revel

in delicacies to be discovered
in garbage cans. Sleep all day.
Develop the wiry muscles

in your pink, prehensile tail:
seeing the world upside down
is sometimes inspiring. Scavenge

country roads, but beware
white lights cascading across
the blacktop. If they approach,

bare all fifty of your teeth.
If that fails to stop them, perform
an Elvis: bask in the electric glow

as you bloat and stiffen; secrete
a horrible smell; hold
perfectly still; and dream

of swallowing the moon.

Prospero in Suburbia

Every day last week when I walked the dogs, I spied an old man in a rusty blue Citron. It was parked in front of Glen Forney's place. The dogs raised their hackles as we passed the car, but the man inside seemed harmless enough. In fact, he was quite friendly. Even though he was busy with stacks of papers, he paused to smile and wave. I asked my wife if she knew the identity of the stranger, and she said it was Glen's father-in-law. He had been kicked out of a retirement home; all he had left was the Citron. My wife said Glen and the father-in-law couldn't stand one another, so the old fellow camped out in his car all day long, going through his papers. At first, I thought he might be reviewing his will— maybe writing Glen out of it. But as I edged closer, day after day, I glimpsed diagrams, hand-colored maps, and charts covered with arcane symbols. Yesterday, I brushed against the driver-side door, barely controlling the howling dogs, and I saw in the old man's lap a blueprint for the elementary school I had attended. His smile was broad as he turned the key to the Citron and said something. Over the rumbling engine and barking dogs, I couldn't hear the words. One day soon, he will open the passenger-side door, and we'll go for a drive together. I'll learn magic, and Glen and my wife won't suspect a damn thing.

Uncracked

Baba Yaga's hut laid a great egg and
would have turned bright red if she could have—
hardly befitting an unnatural terror,
thought the hut, all the sitting still,
the requisite wait for new life;
then there was the question of the father—
that Phoenix who had rushed back to heaven
or the old cock from the village who always
proclaimed his manhood so loudly?

The hut didn't think either would be much
good as a parent, or make the old witch
who lived inside her feel any less bitter
about having her household fixed by
the obligations of motherhood;
the hut settled, tried to comfort herself
with vague memories of what had sat on her
back when she was still vulnerable, before
she became hard both inside and out.

Initiation

During my final year at the house, we made one of the pledges pee on his palms before every social event. We'd snicker in the corners as he shook hands with people he'd just met. Once he was our brother, the hazing stopped—but he didn't. He said the process gave him a psychological edge over strangers. But, he admitted, it didn't work on dates. He asked us again and again what would be the best way to handle new people who might become family.

During a College Production
of Cymbeline

Crimson-masked, Iachimo
emerges long past his cue

after two minutes of
scratching and heaving

against a trunk lid that
refused to open;

while dulcet snores from
Imogen—one wet eye open—

filled the otherwise hushed hall;
while the theatre instructor waited to

blink, and behind her
bright red eyes blazed

visions of the inevitable
review in the student paper.

The nightmare-villain stalls—
one foot in the wooden case,

one foot on the boards—
poised between tragedy averted

and possible mishaps
still to come;

and something pins him
under a green gel,

makes him turn away
from the house, refill

burning lungs, ready himself to
move Up Right, toward

another exposed
wide-awake innocent.

Red-eye Stewardess

Skogsrå in another life,
she circles today
above Cologne—

a familiar tormentor,
despite her plastic visage.
Blood-lips mouth

an ancient spell as she glides
with grace that belies
her broad backside. She tempts

you with little bites—
just enough to remind you
of how you hunger.

Try to sleep away
the interminable night—
yet shimmying hips assault,

rouse you if you slumber.
Cling to one hope:
you need never again

face those too-white teeth
if you safely make it
back to earth.

Another Eviction

Like a late-November fire pit
cobbled together, mother's head filled

with the last leaves and all her private papers—
so many records of unmaking

nobody needed to see. Smoke
clambered up the insides, left behind

greasy fingerprints. The houses next door
spit out a parade of witnesses—

carpenter ants shaken loose
from rotten wood—as what once passed for

life trickled out of chinks everyone missed,
as we watched flames try to escape

walls that would be gone the next day.

Discipline

Rumors of death threats rippled through the lunchroom
following Percy's expulsion. None of us
could imitate a voice we had never heard—

yet we imagined his words had been delivered
through clenched teeth, a Dirty Harry grumble,

like a Rottweiler with a mouth full of white noise.
Even after he returned—still silent as he
skulked through the halls, made himself as small as

the hermit crabs we studied in Biology—
we tittered about switchblades and pipe bombs—

until Percy's older sister told everyone
what had really happened: the English teacher,
Mr. Fiennes, had given Percy a tape recorder

to help him gain confidence for reading
poetry aloud—something called "Howl."

The lines Vice Principal McClinty heard
Percy chanting—screaming, really,
according to McClinty—from a carrel

near the rear of the library, demanded
"immediate sanction." Or so the note

sent home said. After we discovered
the poem online, nobody could figure out
how it should sound, and we wondered

what had happened to the recorded evidence
of the rebellious Percy's real voice.

Tradition and the Individual Talent

The little man with the clip-on-tie cart makes his pitch to everyone who passes: "Never worry about a Shelby or a Windsor; you needn't fret about today's fashions with this contemporary convenience." Nobody listens, so he tries again: "The clip-on tie is democratic, requiring no skill: anyone who can button a shirt can fasten one." Still, nobody stops. He redoubles his efforts: "Neckties are macho; French mercenaries wore them hundreds of years ago. The cravat is really a kind of heraldry, a badge of honor!" Nobody even glances in his direction. Exhausted—and freighted with unsold goods—the little man heaves a sigh and packs up. As he steers his cart with one unsteady hand, he slides the other into his pocket and weaves his fingers through a balled-up, dirty bowtie.

After the Buyout

Our last week was devoted to changing
clocks. As we shuffled from empty room
to empty room, we swapped

swinging hands cased in steel
for digital displays. We did not
waste breath. But on break
we buzzed about plans

for the weeks ahead, unpacking
daydreams and store-brand
peanut butter crackers. Perched

on the edges of metal
folding chairs, we debated
how best to employ the time:
rip apart our rotten decks, tear off

asphalt shingles, or take down
dying trees behind our homes? The volume
increased as we rehearsed acts of demolition—

yet we were careful to keep
our faces angled toward our laps,
reluctant to see what might be
stuck between our teeth.

As Above

When white oak seedlings bloom
in gutters, I leave them alone:

hapless new lives, nowhere

to lay down roots, nowhere
to go but up toward heaven.

Still, I dream one morning

I might wake to find
tendrils snaking through

AC vents to caress my cheek

as thanks for the reprieve—
or to remind me of just how

far from the sun I dwell.

Semiotics

Susan, the little girl who never goes to school, stands at the edge of her yard all morning long. She knows not to go into the street. Yet she knows too she will not get into trouble if she lets her shadow pass beyond the yard. With the tips of her toes, she pushes down the blades of grass that border the street and inches forward to let her darkness sprawl across the pavement. On the other side of the street, three Jack Russell terriers race back and forth, rattling a metal fence. They seem to call Susan—she tries her best to understand. To let them know she hears, she shouts back "barr, barr, barr," repeatedly pitching the syllable where she will never go. The animals ignore her but continue to cry out to her shadow, which trembles just a few inches beyond the boundary that keeps them all from running wild.

Sons of Adam

Every afternoon when we lived on Beagle Street, two old men circled our block. Each began his constitutional on a street parallel to ours. They started in opposite directions, yet invariably came face-to-face. Although I never saw them speak, the one approaching from the south always gave a quick wave—a sharp judo chop—when he spied the opposing figure. His counterpart kept his gaze locked on the pavement before him—as though one misstep might send him spiraling into the abyss. But when the two drew close enough to touch, the man from the north raised his eyes, then nodded. After studying the routine for a few weeks, I started to call the former figure The Diplomat, the latter The Bookkeeper. When my brother learned about the labels, he insisted that I was foolish for caring about personal names. The men must be related, he laughed, punctuating his point with a sudden slap to my jaw. The family connection was what really mattered.

X-ray Vision

No word in the comic book ads
    of headaches, eyestrain, or doubling—

I'd have ordered the glasses anyhow,
    hoping to penetrate the body's mysteries.

When my wife saw me wearing them,
    I hoped she would laugh along.

I grinned and rubbed my pounding
    temples, waited expectantly.

Her look pierced me, extended toward
    a place far beyond our home.

She started to unbutton and sighed,
    You simply should have asked.

Flicker

After all my deliberate listening,
I never once caught the staccato
drum beat—only saw evidence

my stepfather pointed out: scores
of pits and pocks round the door frame—
as though the bird was desperate

to get inside. Everybody had a theory
about why she wanted to burrow
into our suburban shell:

mom worried loggers had destroyed
a nest while harvesting nearby woods;
my brother believed pests secreted

in plaster provoked the attack;
grandmother felt the visitor a sign—
of what she didn't know. Reasons

mattered little to my stepfather
when weighed against his desire
to repair what had been

done to the façade. He told me
how he wrapped the trim
in thick reflective tape, and I

envisioned the bird on her last visit
sinking her bill into the sticky stuff,
trembling as her wings flapped—

the arms of a conductor
without an orchestra. My stepfather
bragged about how he took

care of the threat, but nobody
wanted to believe—especially after
the damage was done.

Hives

Half-finished, after Hurricane Frances
rattled branch to root, some will remain

a little while longer—until
some starving raccoon splits them open,

or a mower crushes them beneath
black rubber wheels: paper

rounds dotting the lawn, swirling grey
as durable as dreams. I wade through

the wreckage of bark and acorns,
of leaves and limbs. My unscathed roof

makes me bold enough to prod
one sphere with a toe, risk an attack

from diamond-backed lancers. The fallen nation
disgorges only a queen. With stately slowness,

she drags herself across the debris, not quite
ready to ascend, to begin again to build

a home that might forever hang in air.

Once Jolly Green Giant

It's not envy
that made me
like this—

just a job,
like every other one,
filled with compromise.

Once upon a time,
I was red. Used
to eat burgers daily.

Steaks every weekend.
Holiday feasts
of little men

who had followed
some bean stalk
or magical staircase

to my palace in the sky—
then I grew too heavy
to dwell in clouds,

far above
the world of TV
and canned goods.

Today I live under
a contract,
always displaying

blunted teeth,
no longer able to
eat meat.

Stress Interview

Once the door locked, she became
a map: proxy for mile upon mile of terrain,
under swirling colors, below the palms

of an overzealous meteorologist.
She felt him track a nasty southbound system—
so many semaphores to articulate

the scope of imminent disaster
rolling across the country. She thought
everyone should know enough to stay

out of harm's way, hidden in a basement—
but some folks never do listen to
warnings: some folks have to work.

Pitch

As in summers past, asphalt spread
like a virus up and down the lane:
the new couple at the north end
renewed the black urge,
sealed a drive just one year old;

the banker who is never home followed—
antimatter spilled across
his double-wide roundabout, threatened
to swallow his Hummer whole. Others
soon were hooked again, tried

to keep up with the dark rage:
the retired couple catty-corner,
the French teacher in the fixer-upper.
Every day fresh tar fumes
penetrated our bedroom

along with memories of dinosaur tombs
we had visited on our honeymoon.
Nostalgia aside, I knew the new
surfaces didn't matter:
mere oil and water,

so much cheap makeup smeared
over deep pockmarks,
the sealant didn't do anything
about the damage down below.
Still, I started to imagine

my tires might tear or my feet
might snag as I walked to the mailbox,
and after a week with too little sleep—
waking daily to the smell

of envy, waste, and history—
I admitted to a neighbor
I needed a number I had
misplaced, to call the tar guys
we all used for a fix.

Lapses

My sister always threw away my plastic snakes—
once she stopped screaming. After I lost a particu-
larly choice southern ringneck that had been secret-
ed under her pillow, I decided to glue the next snake
in place. But as I prepared an eastern hognose
for her sock drawer, some glue stuck to my palm,
which then stuck to the snake. Unable to get free of
him, I panicked, worried I'd be caught sabotaging
my sister's hosiery. I shoved my fist—clutching the
snake—deep inside my pocket, where both remained
throughout the day. That evening, the snake began
to squirm. It whispered to me in sibilant tones: "It's
warm down here. I think I'll stay. We'll be together
forever." I knew from Sunday school that snakes of-
ten lied. But I wasn't sure about plastic ones—not
even after sweat broke down the adhesive and I re-
moved my empty hand from my still-rustling pocket.

Ancient History

After the trial, Xanthippe torched
the books she had preserved
during decades of marriage—

ledgers to track love owed her, shared
with Athens; survival guides
she shoved before him, hoping

to keep him off the flypaper. He had
no library, wanted no tracks—
though his course to Philopappou was

marked by many. She wished she had
a record of his philosophy
to burn. He meant never to be

reduced to smudges on disciples'
fingers. She was a sea beast
that used ink to disappear.

She never told about the poetry
she wrote during their first days together,
when she believed in words,

back when he used them like a mallet
and chisel to remove excess
hiding the shape of her spirit.

Artist Statements

Behind the gas station, I passed
through the pink door—

the only one unlocked—
minutes later, emerged to collide

with a flint-jawed old woman
and a teary-eyed little girl.

Toward the blue door, now ajar,
I motioned; tried to say something

funny: I hadn't plucked the flowers
from the pretty wallpaper

or overturned the potpourri—
but as I started to deliver excuses

the little girl hissed a curse
and I swallowed all the words I knew

later would turn my stomach.

Half-beast

Almost undone, my brother
confessed he had tasted the breath

of the lamia: wet and sweet,

like rosé just uncorked, powerful
enough to make the temples

throb. He admitted he had

gazed for hours into pools
of bottomless night, never

rippling, despite the stories

of men drowning there.
I asked why he couldn't

just find a neighborhood girl,

reminded him he'd been hurt before
by such exotic creatures.

He protested she was misunderstood:

his lover did not devour every man—
besides, you could have one hell of a time

if you brought her fresh-cut flowers;

it wasn't like in those tall tales,
he smirked: her bottom half was just fine.

I haven't seen him for almost a year now—

last heard she'd lured him back east
to live among other monsters.

Baba Yaga As Figure Model

Only for a moment after the robe dropped
did the ancient witch feel chilled. As she shut
her eyes, felt sun soak through her thin skin,

listened to brushstrokes fill the emptiness
like a child's bedtime prayer, she could smell
the pungent acrylics—then began to doze.

One student alone marked the thin trail
of spittle glistening in canyons
scored around the harridan's eel-like lips

while the rest of class struggled to trace
the barbed wire wrapped around her spine.
Her old lungs rattled like an air conditioner

as she cooed in dreams at a Toltecan god
who waltzed on giant chicken legs,
her eyes aflutter, just as they had been

the first time she revealed herself to another—
and nobody captured the interplay of light
and darkness underneath her frosted brow.

Middle-age As a Mailbox

The hand of authority
daily puts itself inside
my hollow head,
far from formal
but leery of spiderwebs
deep in the back.

Sometimes I wonder
if it would be better
to remain empty, unstuffed
with reminders,
sealed and stamped,
of duties unwanted.

Wish I knew how to
abandon my post,
how to keep down
my faded red flag—
how to keep
my big mouth shut.

On Spotting Your Second Ex-husband

A grenade pin pulled, your hand

dropped from mine,
and from under shielded eyes

I spied seas

heaving up
a barge long ago sunk

by unscrupulous buccaneers

purple-eyed and rum-drunk
as waves of unsavory memory

crashed over our tomorrow.

Instructions for My Stunt Double

You won't have to hang
from hoods of speeding cars.

I admit there might be a fall
or two,

an entrance
through a closed door—

what you'd expect
from the type of part

I usually play.
There was a time—

but then I'm not
as tall as I used to be.

Dates, family holidays, and showers
at the gym, all present liabilities.

I don't want to
jeopardize the production.

Any lines in the scenes
you can mouth;

a voice will later be laid in.
Be sure to get the costumes

just so—
then position yourself far, far

away from everyone:
make your true face

blur.

Community Arts

The night we decided to try a new approach to vandalism was my idea. Instead of amputating car mirrors and decapitating lawn ornaments, we would destroy the official identities of everyone in the neighborhood. Cloaked in sable hoodies, we clutched flashlights and glue as we crept from house to house. First, we ripped the characters off each mailbox; then we rearranged them. "Leon Hoster" metamorphosized into "HoLe stoner." "The Cheneys" transformed into "yes Then Che." It took almost all night to make our way around the block, but I was sure the payoff would make the hard work worthwhile: come morning, chaos would ensue. Yet the next day, most folks didn't seem to notice what had been done to them—at least not until late in the day, when they picked up the usual loads of bills and junk mail, after work. Before the sun dropped that evening, more than half the characters had been rearranged into their original configurations, and within three days, everyone was back to normal. The other boys complained about wasting so much time without results. But I convinced them they shouldn't have listened to me in the first place—as if manipulating a bunch of letters ever really mattered.

Midway

Clamped between jaws, halfway inside
        and out, she doesn't know how

she fell into this trap before
        the workday began: no room

for her door to open, a wall
        on the other side too;

the little motor above groaning
        like it's giving birth;

the garage door straining to reach
        the familiar resting place

below. Nothing happens, again,
        as she pumps the gas, tries

to remember exactly when she hit
        the button, but can't pinpoint

the moment her mind split—
        a chicken bone half-full of luck—

unready to face what should have been
      finished at the office yesterday,

focused on all that needed to be left
      undone at home today.

Lost in Amish Country

Yesterday loses some
of its gilded luster

when you are stuck

in traffic on the way
to Dutch Wonderland—

almost one hour behind

a horse-drawn
black buggy, nothing

to look at but fields

and the occasional
outlet mall; bad

lines make the cell

no good and on
the satellite radio

nothing comes through

you haven't heard
one thousand times

before—so you listen

to road noise, old and
new: the shrill squeal

of your tired brakes

and the regular crack
of hooves belonging to

a horse you can't see.

Last Bus to Hell

Afraid he'd never find someone
able to stand fetid breath like a compost heap,
a temper quick to snap like a flag in a gale,
Cerberus cried when he spied the Greyhound
before the black gates of hell. She
slammed him harder than Hercules had:
and it wasn't just her size that impressed,
led him to abandon his post, to give chase—
the hellhound couldn't resist the cool,
smooth surfaces of a painted femme fatale.

Another Eris

This poem began while I was part of a group that professed aesthetic nihilism. The woman who founded the group taught philosophy at a local university. She proposed to gather us weekly throughout the spring to write. At the end of the season, we would burn everything we had produced. She asserted that destruction of the lie that is expression is the only form of truth. I told her she was onto something inspiring.

Richard of Gloucester's Machine

Imperfect the time—
or perhaps you know

me, not for chitchat,

called while I was absent,
to avoid my untamed

temper, my wicked wit;

flying through my throat
like hungry kites,

both make me unhappy

to create—unhappier still to
hear—this message,

my voice a spur

to prick me to forget
myself; yet should you

wish to address something

to my person, to get
in touch another time,

an electronic cue marks

the waiting
emptiness now—

Pared

When Myra confessed she had a twin, unseen
for years and years—a Mary—who

in a high school production of tales by Ovid
once played Narcissus with her

as the radiant pool of deadly seduction,
I insisted nobody could be so pretty.

When she turned aside, didn't smile
as I'd hoped, I rankled; charged her

with vanity; pried and pushed—
until Myra finally revealed she first

chose me as a lover because Mary had
long ago swallowed her self-esteem,

and ever since she secretly felt
she only rated second best. As I

fought to catch my breath, I saw
she was as perfect as glass.

The Love Song of Tick-Tock Croc

I want to be a white whale,
trade rough green scales
for smooth clean skin;
become a blank page,
ready for another to
imprint a story upon me.

I want to be a white whale—
no clock tolling deep inside,
a reminder of mortality, to make me
wonder how long I'll last
in Neverland, my dance partner
obsessed with booty and punctilio.

I want to be a white whale
with my own Ahab—inflamed,
ready to grapple to the last,
bent on getting hooks in me—
to be pursued, perhaps succumb,
before a hunter's hot heart bursts!

Teaching Hamlet *at St. Egwin's School for Girls*

He pretends he is not competing
with hot electric words, half-hidden in plaid

folds in their laps, as he attempts again
to rescue poor Polonius—dismissed

by his students for hypocrisy, a sin he has
come to regard as venial. "Brevity,"

he declaims once more, "is the soul of wit."
If windy, obtuse, and a little delusory,

the counselor is, after all, a fellow teacher—
his advice to Laertes fundamentally sound.

He elicits nothing but sighs and
rolled eyes from the girls, who do not want to listen

to a cross, old man insisting that the rich boy,
clad in black, need not always steal the show.

Transparent

Mary kept her photos spread across the top of a wine crate, under a piece of oversized glass. We'd rest our drinks on skinnier, happier versions of her arm in arm with old beaus. I couldn't avoid inserting myself into those old scenes, imagining myself with another her—at prom or a county fair. During one of our last fights, as I threw up a hand in frustration, I caught it on a corner of the glass. She cried as blood dripped onto the pictures and I loudly cursed the glass. But when she began to clean up, she murmured: "That's exactly what it's there for."

Cyclopean

Blindness has begun
in both eyes, doctors say,

but the left looks

far worse than the right.
Perhaps I am fated to become

a hero in a Greek tragedy,

only half-seeing the world.
Leery of monsters

I might be obliged

to stand before,
I have fixed blurry sights

on a machine-made replica—

glass to replace
the failing organ. Until

I need a match

for the other side,
this single undilating orb

must do—make me appear

normal enough to hold
the Furies at bay.

Casting

From between toppled logs, spider legs
    and mouse droppings spill as downed wood
        again falls like fate, and I prepare

to rebuild the woodpile. Scanning
    the shambles, I seek a catch to release
        the base row, sunken into the ground,

committed to ripening in this place:
    the rotten logs must be wrestled loose,
        carted into deep woods to be forgotten.

I know from years past they won't go
    without a fight with the living, clinging
        to muddy March ground, as if to suggest

the recently dead dream of roots.

Strapped

When she couldn't get to sleep, the little girl would ask her father to tell her a story. He was a widower, and he cared about her more than anything—even more than himself—so he always indulged her. Nevertheless, the little girl was often unhappy and frequently sleepless. One night, when she was particularly restless, after her father had failed to calm her with an old tale about Baba Yaga, she insisted on telling him a new story. It was called "Strapped," and it featured a mummy with nothing inside its white swaddling layers. The hollow mummy had generally bad prospects. He drank too much, and when under the influence, he'd start to unravel his own limbs. He also liked to set fires; he'd nearly burned himself up twice last month. People from a local museum wanted to lock up the mummy in a case—like some mannequin in a department store window. They said it was for his own good. The widower confessed he didn't like the story very much, but he felt bad for the mummy. Don't, replied his daughter: if you knew him back when he was alive, you'd think he deserved even worse.

Why, Iago?

Because of falling
        markets.

Because of rising
        costs.

Because I feel myself
        a vestigial Vice.

Because I don't ask
        or tell.

Because I didn't
        take Viagra.

Because I took
        too much Viagra.

Because of the plot
        of *Un Capitano Moro.*

Because kids today
        don't know anything.

Because of all the sex
        and violence on TV.

Claws

Resolved to keep his vow, unstretch

the likeness of balmy thighs sweeping up
toward chthonic mysteries secreted

in her center, skin purer than canvas

before he touched it with his brush,
masked coarseness under layers of love,

he finally finds he cannot make himself

remove his former mistress from the frame—
instead decides to keep her always

close, underneath the gold and azure

of a sunrise never witnessed, where
he prays she will remain forever

safe from his wife's sharp critiques.

Ex Nihilo

One of the last times we visited my wife's mother at the rest home, the old lady reported she'd been robbed: "They stole my shoes. They stole my sweaters. They stole my memories." At first we thought the octogenarian's mind was playing tricks on her. However, an inventory of her apartment revealed that, while all the shoes were present, several sweaters were indeed missing. So we decided to mount a security camera above her door, to catch the thieves in the act. But on our next visit, the camera was gone. My wife's mother maintained it too had been stolen. Eventually, she whimpered, everything would be taken from her. Resolved to get to the bottom of the mystery, we purchased another camera and secreted it in a begonia my mother-in-law kept by the window. We could hardly wait to examine the evidence when we returned the next morning. Only my wife's mother was gone. Nobody had seen her leave, and no visitors had signed the logbook. Luckily, our begonia-cam was present, so we immediately hooked it up to her television set. As playback began, my wife's mother appeared napping in a chair. Then—just like that—she vanished. When I turned to ask my wife if she had witnessed the event, she too had disappeared. I never have determined if my wife was stolen or if the eradication of her mother simply made it too hard for her to exist. Either way, I have the begonia and the second camera as evidence of her being.

Unburied

Here is how granddaddy explained
his original family: Goodwin
had been with him since before
he settled down, but his first wife balked
when he announced the dog would be
buried in the pasture where he loved
to bound and play. She scoffed:
the winter ground was harder
than any of granddaddy's tools—
if not his head. Without another word,
he set to work with his blowtorch, created
a fissure in which he planted a stick
of dynamite usually reserved for summer
stump removal. The fuse flickered
while granddaddy ducked for cover—
then a howl from the underworld
rattled the glass between the house
and the untamed outdoors. Confetti
of earth and ice and flame whirled
through the air, along with Goodwin's secrets:
gnawed bones and sticks and a lone lady's boot
whose mate had been discarded years before—
reserves for a dog day that would never come.
When the air cleared, Goodwin was
lowered into the space, the gravedigger
alone as witness. Granddaddy's first wife
had turned away, didn't speak again

for the remainder of winter—
not one syllable until after
seasons changed and a great stone
rolled from the woods marked where
Goodwin rested: an awkward reminder
like the ones at roadside accidents.

Samhain

You can hang despair
on the gun hooks—

drilled into our walls
by former owners—

after the sun drops,
like Newton's apple

filled with sin
and razor blades.

Entanglements

Invisible nets bar the way between
the oaks, above ground I rarely mow.

They crisscross the yard, bind
tree to tree—as though the spiders feel

obliged to hold everything together.
Or perhaps they hope to correct

crooked routes the limbs take
toward sunlight; or drag unruly

woods back to earth. Everywhere
unseen threads speak to a vision

too broad for one pair of eyes.
Atop my John Deere, I never spy

webs before I feel them upon my face—
and as the machine continues to roll

beneath me, I worry
the strands won't break.

Another Labyrinth

The old hero clutched a massive, bloody head by its horns as he staggered into the kitchen. Raising his prize with a grunt, he plopped it onto the table, where his wife was dicing onions. "My dear, I've finally slain the Minotaur!" he declared. She eyed the gory trophy for a moment, before narrowing her dark eyes. "How do I know," she snorted, "this doesn't belong to some bull?" Just then, the head released a long, low chortle that made the golden ring in its nose jangle. Holding her paring knife before her, the woman slowly backed away from the table. As the head continued to laugh, the old hero addressed his wife through clenched teeth: "Must you always make a mystery out of what's not there?"

Athena Calling

Invisible, the creature captured me
with a barrage of questions

halfway through the night; wrenched me

away from moonlight and the red glow
of the clock, the warm body

beside me, the heavy breathing

of the dogs ringed round our bed;
drew me toward the cold caliginosity

of the other side

of the house. Fumbling through
the study door, I again heard

the predator proclaim himself,

unanswered. No light penetrated
the back windows

below cloud-pricking pines,

and I groped toward the couch,
where I found an old blanket to

serve as shroud; stretched out

and slowed my spirit;
head perfectly still, while

I waited for another sleep.

Reception

That summer when my sister first came home from college, she brought with her a blind rabbit she found by the roadside. My sister loved the classics, so she named the rabbit Homer. When she went to work at the restaurant in evenings, Homer stayed in the living room, in front of our television. It was always on in those days, even though lines marred the picture. As Homer listened to the noise, his ears twitched like the hands of two kids vying for the attention of their teacher. The television kept its ears still while classics flashed across its face. Late at night, after my sister returned home, she would turn off the television and read to Homer. Mostly she picked stuff from her college classes, like Dante, Shakespeare, and Melville. Homer loved to hear her voice, and his ears danced as she read, undulating until she couldn't hold back her laughter. The week before my sister had to go back to school, she brought Homer to a local animal shelter. The people there said they'd take care of him. For five nights straight, I could hear my sister crying through the wall between our rooms, no matter how tightly I clamped a pillow over my ears. And I knew then that there wasn't going to be anything on television worth watching that fall.

Company Cookout

Unseeing, bats don't care
about layoffs and morale

as they dive
through purple skies

after the hum
of myriad bodies

filling the air—
while below we rub

smoke from red eyes
and show our teeth

to the boss, pretending
we are not being

eaten alive.

Erosion

After the April rains,
giant anthills always erupt
next door. Only I know

they are not fashioned
by bugs. Before dawn,
invisible machines rumble

between the houses,
shake us from slumber,
deposit loads of topsoil

to restore what has been
washed away. It's costly,
I suspect, but never ask

what the neighbors pay.
But I worry about where
all the fill comes from,

imagine a growing void
out there in the wild—beyond
our artificial landscapes.

Improvident

Untouched, two lone survivors cleaved

to roosting rods, above the wet crimson
mess smeared across the planks. Why

they were spared by the red

fox who had carried chaos indoors—
their sisters away—remained

a mystery; the reason

didn't really matter: the girls
never recovered, and after

the eggs stopped, we couldn't

read the poems scratched
in the dirt; they couldn't

understand our apology

when we brought them
behind the corn crib to

the chopping block.

The Second Furlough

Lunch made out of habit, headed nowhere,
rests on the kitchen countertop, beside
a flip-toy dog who never lands on his feet
no matter how hard his windup is cranked.

Even sprung on the living room carpet,
he must feel the impact as he crashes down
on head or haunch; and before you return
to bed, you can't help but think

about the breaking bones—even though
they must have been removed long ago,
so small children wouldn't swallow them
if they spilled out of the inevitable cracks.

If I Were a Woman

Rumors swirled about another stunt—
like last season's Zen rock garden as Rome—
a female Adam reeked of flash and politics.

When asked about his creative vision,
the director merely shrugged;
he didn't share how auditions had

seemed to redress tradition—
too few men, too many women.
All the unpleasant chatter changed

to plaudits after opening night:
Adam's frosted beard stayed in place
through numerous scenes of hand-wringing;

and more importantly, the performer
delighted in each luculent syllable,
as though savoring some great bounty.

Nobody even noticed how Orlando suffered
when shouldering his servant, trying not
to touch delicate parts.

Baba Yaga's Yard Sale

Tired of haggling over dimes
and nickels for VHS tapes,
she gives up her collection
for just two bucks. A young couple
inspects a lamp made from the skull
of a Moroccan prince
who dared hunt witches,
filling dark steppes with trumpet song—
then screams. The couple sneers
at the five-dollar price tag.
The lovers stalk back to their Hummer.
Nobody has even looked at the elliptical
that cost two hundred new,
and the witch suspects she should have
wiped away the dust before
she dragged it up those steep
basement steps. Soon she will be
obliged to cart the bike back
underground—along with all
her other unsold goods: stacks
of *Women's Fitness*, a juicer
still in the box, three pairs of bat wings.
Baba Yaga exhales, fondling
an incomplete set of nesting dolls—
missing its outermost shell, diminished
despite the bright lives hidden inside—
overpriced at fifty cents.

Dualism

The man in the squirrel suit woke me from an uneasy
sleep. I heard him digging in the backyard, and his
hole was so deep that I could only glimpse his sleek
grey ears—until I drew close. I stood there watching
him rip into the ground and hurl up earth. While I
was annoyed at being awakened, I was impressed
by his ability to break up the hard ground. When
he noticed me, he paused and turned his stygian
eyes toward mine. I thought it might be my neighbor,
Glen Forney, inside the getup. But I didn't want to
ruin the moment, so instead of asking who was in
the costume I asked what he wanted in the ground.
"Treasures long ago forgotten." When he replied, his
tail twitched, as though passing electric current up
to his mouth. It sure didn't sound like Glen's voice. I
tried to be more specific with my next question and
asked if he was looking for nuts. Yet the man in the
squirrel suit had gone back to digging, and I realized
I wasn't going to get anything more out of him. I
suddenly felt very tired and wanted nothing so much
as to stop this racket and return to bed. It was too
late to call my pest control guys, so I headed toward
my garage, thinking I'd get a shovel to end this nui-
sance. Only after I flipped on the lights in the garage
and started to rummage through my tools did I real-
ize that the shovel was missing: I'd lent it to Glen, a
few months ago, and he'd never returned it.

Marked

I don't know why uncle Tommy decided to take off his shirt at that Fourth of July picnic. Probably we kids egged him on, asking him to show more freckles. He always told us stories about them, bragging that each freckle captured the profile of something he'd killed. He would roll up his pant legs to his knees, all of us ringed around him. A fallen deer stood near his left ankle, a raccoon on his left calf, and a wild boar on his right thigh. A bunch of squirrels scaled his shins, and he had matching opossums on his knees. When he bared his torso that day, the list of victims grew: he showed us slain bison and zebra, murdered wolves and lions. He promised to reveal a special freckle, but only if we swore ourselves to secrecy. Right below his navel, he put his finger beside a freckle he said represented Nancy, his ex-wife. I was pretty sure I had seen her with her new husband at the Food Lion the week before. But Tommy maintained he had done her in, just like the other victims dotting his skin. My cousin Susie was not convinced: she insisted the profile looked like her mother and started to cry. Tommy might have been able to control the situation even then, but my little brother, Hector, thought the freckle actually resembled him. Before Tommy could say anything, Hector ran screaming toward the other adults, wailing that Tommy planned to kill him. I remember now I thought the face looked a little like Tommy's, though I can't be sure—I haven't seen him for such a long time.

Caroline Fox Considers Jeremy Bentham's Proposal (1805)

She could not forget how after
a stalemate game of chess
fifteen years before

she was ready to swallow
whatever he concocted—so long
as they stayed in the dark.

Yet he had refused to be drawn
from the well-lit path, under
the canopy of pines marking

the edge of order. Right
out in the open, he pulped
her ripe lips. Better to have all

exposed, he murmured,
even as she continued to tug him
toward seclusion. He held

fast, greedy hands
fumbling, eyes closed—
no faculty of knowledge

in him. Now she planted
herself, rejected a lifetime
of choices pinched

like market fruit—
under the fingers of strangers
seeking rot, no matter

how brilliant the colors.

Secret Recipe

One day a widow found a dead raccoon in front of her home. It looked fresh, so she snatched it, intending to make a stew. She was surprised when the raccoon suddenly turned and bit her leg. But you're dead, she protested. I learned that trick from a possum, muttered the raccoon, who still had the widow's leg gripped between his teeth. That's unfair, the widow complained. You've been living alone far too long, countered the raccoon. With that he let go of the widow's leg and removed his black mask. Look you, said the widow, I don't care who you are. There's still tonight's dinner to think of.

The Second Separation

Knees and palms smeared red, she
swiveled in her mother's velvety arms,

shot a look of disbelief toward

the mulberry that had refused
to crook its limbs, to return

her embrace, releasing her

pinwheeling to the ground.
Did she see, her mother

murmured, the tree only cared

about itself, about touching
the divine? This is the story

she told me when I asked

why she was leaving. She never believed
we were free to bend and stand at once,

to rise and fall together, before
she went to bleed her features

once more into her mother's sleeves.

Katabasis

It started with a lie about a tunnel
leading to buried treasure. After
my brother lured me out back

to inspect the little hole he had started,
he urged me to help mine it.
Once the opening reached down

two feet, he declared we deserved a break,
said hard work rated rewards, explained
people on vacations covered themselves

with dirt all the time. I knew better
but didn't complain as he directed me
into the opening, then began to blanket me

under layers of sod. I didn't say a thing
when he revised his story: this was
a dress rehearsal for my burial—

an event he had been anticipating
for years and years. I knew I could say nothing
to change his course, so kept my mouth closed

as soil encircled my chin like a dark collar.
Through gritted teeth, I could taste
the earth: wet pennies on my tongue.

Once my brother finished, he waved
goodbye, and it was a relief
to be alone, unable to move;

it was warm in the ground, like being
in a sleeping bag, and I began to
lose feeling in my limbs. I fantasized

about life as a bodiless head—
no toes to be stepped on,
no arms to be pinched—

and in my cerebral haze I began to doze,
almost in ecstasy, falling under
the spell of sleep—

until I remembered the neighborhood dogs
roamed free every evening, imagined
this might truly become an interminable holiday.

Everything I had tried to forget
erupted, sent hot blood pounding up
into my head, and I began to sing,

keening like Orpheus in a voice
I hoped would be powerful enough to
help me escape the underworld.

Ritual to Romance

Nobody in the development at the top of the hill pays attention to the apple farm below—until the end of fall. Every year, in the middle of November, the farmers erect an altar to the coming winter: a burn pile made of harvest waste. As smoke thick enough to rest a martini on rolls into the development, it seems as though it should set off all the car alarms and rouse the guard dogs. But the miasma makes no sound, and it leaves no footprints on the fresh-cut lawns while it slides between the exfoliated trees, rubbing them up and down like a shoeshine rag. If you are caught outside and chance to look up, for an instant it appears the leaves have returned: limbs no longer naked, draped in pumice robes, quiver, ready to provide a sign. You wonder if you will be able to keep your watery eyes open to see which way the gnarled fingers point. And you practice holding your breath.

About the Author

Noel Sloboda is the author of the poetry collection *Shell Games* (sunnyoutside, 2008) as well as several chapbooks, most recently *Circle Straight Back* (Červená Barva Press, 2012). He has also published a book about Edith Wharton and Gertrude Stein. Sloboda teaches at Penn State York and serves as dramaturg for the Harrisburg Shakespeare Company.